DEAR BRIDE

Dear Bride

Letters from Jesus, the Bridegroom, to His Betrothed

RACHEL WENKE

By Rachel Wenke

Copyright © 2020 by Rachel Wenke

All rights reserved. No part of this book may be reproduced in any manner without written permission except in the case of brief quotations embodied in articles and reviews.

First Printing, 2020, Australia.
For more information about this book or author please visit:
www.KnowingGod.life

All Scripture quotations unless otherwise indicated, are taken from the New King James Version®. Copyright © 1982, Thomas Nelson, Inc. Used by permission. All rights reserved. Scripture quotations marked (ESV) are from The ESV® Bible (The Holy Bible, English Standard Version®), copyright © 2001 by Crossway, a publishing ministry of Good News Publishers. Used by permission. All rights reserved. Scripture quotations marked TPT are from The Passion Translation®. Copyright © 2017, 2018 by Passion & Fire Ministries, Inc. Used by permission. All rights reserved. ThePassionTranslation.com.

Cover photo by Sabrinna Ringquist

Contents

Preface — vii

Letter 1: True Fulfilment — 11
Letter 2: Preparing A Place — 15
Letter 3: You Are My Betrothed — 19
Letter 4: An Eternal Marriage — 23
Letter 5: Experiencing Heaven On Earth — 27
Letter 6: How I See You — 31
Letter 7: Living As One — 35
Letter 8: Besotted By You — 39
Letter 9: You Are My Bride — 43
Letter 10: My Kiss — 47
Letter 11: The Place Beyond Words — 51
Letter 12: I Am Returning For You — 55
Invitation To A New Life With Jesus — 61
Other Books By This Author — 67

Preface

For your Maker is your husband,
The Lord of hosts is His name

Isaiah 54:5

Throughout Scripture, Jesus is referred to as our Husband or Bridegroom, and the body of believers - the Church, as His Bride. This includes all believers, both men and women alike.

The following series of love letters, addressed to His Bride, was inspired by the Holy Spirit, to draw you closer to Jesus so you may receive a deeper revelation of His love for you.

Take your time slowly reading each of these letters. For many of you, you will feel drawn to read some of the letters many times so that you may receive the truths God wants to impart to you more deeply.

As you open your heart to receive the words, it is God's desire that you are drawn into greater oneness and intimacy with your beloved Bridegroom, Jesus Christ. His love is truly the greatest treasure you will ever know.

*And to the husbands,
you are to demonstrate
love for your wives with
the same tender
devotion that Christ
demonstrated to us,
his bride.*

Ephesians 5:25 (TPT)

Letter 1: True Fulfilment

And the Spirit and the bride say, "Come!" And let him who hears say, "Come!" And let him who thirsts come. Whoever desires, let him takethe water of life freely.

Revelation 22:17

Dear Bride,

Why do you strive to gain the world's accolades and accomplishments when the greatest accomplishment and success you will ever know is living in union with Me? Why are you searching and pursuing the world when I am waiting here to be pursued and sought by you? Your Maker, Your Husband, I am waiting for you, My Bride.

Why do you try to draw life from things of this earth and wonder why you feel so empty inside? Why do you continue to draw satisfaction and worth from the opinions of others and wonder why you feel something in your life is missing?

You will always have a sense of emptiness and hollowness inside of you the more you draw life from things apart from My love for you. You see the more you draw from things outside of Me, the more My very life seems to escape you and the "void" inside will begin to be known. The more you turn to Me, Your Bridegroom, and feast on My love and draw from My life, the more fullness, peace and joy you will experience.

Know My love, every time you draw away from Me to the world's fleeting pleasures, emptiness and heartache will soon follow. Let your heart rather be full with My love and My grace towards you. Dwell on Me and My love for you precious Bride, for the pleasures within Me are not fleeting, they are eternal. Dwell on the riches of My glory I have in store for you in oneness and union with Me. Turn your eyes to Me and be filled. Live your life in oneness and union with Me and experience true fulfilment.

Letter 2: Preparing A Place

In My Father's house are many rooms. If it were not so, would I have told you that I go to prepare a place for you?

John 14:2-3 (ESV)

Letter 2: Preparing A Place

Dear Bride,

Do you know that even now as you go about your day and cares of this world I am busy preparing a room for you in glory? You can only imagine the delights and infinite treasures I have stored up in heaven My Bride, awaiting you in My Father's house. It brings Me great delight to prepare this room just for you, for you to delight in when we meet for our wedding feast.

You will take great joy in experiencing all the wonder of what I have prepared, for it is hand-fashioned just for you; for your tastes, your likes, and your unique ways and for no one else. Because you, My Bride, are one of a kind. There is no one in all creation whom I made like you.

I made you specifically for a purpose which I planned for you to fulfil before the foundation of the earth. And as I wait in eager anticipation for you to return to Me, as you go about fulfilling the good works I have prepared for you, so I keep preparing this room for you. Do you want to see it?

Yet, I know while you will take great joy in feasting with your senses all that I have prepared for you, it will not come close to the bliss you will experience in meeting Me face to face in glory. This is the day I am counting down to see fulfilled- the day you come to live with Me forever in glory.

Letter 3: You Are My Betrothed

I will betroth you to Me forever;
Yes, I will betroth you to Me
In righteousness and justice,
In lovingkindness and mercy;
I will betroth you to Me
in faithfulness,
And you shall know the Lord.

Hosea 2:19

Letter 3: You Are My Betrothed

Dear Bride,

Do you know what it means to be betrothed? It means we are bound by a covenant to be wed. You are My Bride and I am your Bridegroom, yet the wedding feast has not yet been. We are in a covenant of marriage that will be consummated in all its fullness in glory.

Yet, you do not need to wait until heaven to experience being My Bride. You are My Bride now, today.

When you surrendered your heart to Me, you entered a covenant. You became My betrothed and I became your Betrothed. I became yours and you became Mine.

Like a promise is sealed with a ring; I sealed this covenant, this union of ours, with My very own blood and nothing or no one can come between us. You are promised to Me forever.

Letter 3: You Are My Betrothed

Letter 4: An Eternal Marriage

Marriage is the beautiful design of the Almighty, a great and sacred mystery—meant to be a vivid example of Christ and his church.

Ephesians 3:32 (TPT)

Letter 4: An Eternal Marriage

Dear Bride,

You may experience an earthly marriage here on earth and delight in becoming one with the partner I have prepared for you but this earthly union will always be a shadow of the eternal union I have with you, My Bride.

Earthly marriage is glorious for I created it but it is never to be an idol or lorded over Me for it is fleeting. It is only of this earth. Your marriage to Me is eternal. It will never end. It will endure for all eternity. As you leave this earthly life, it will continue forever in heaven.

So enjoy the gift of marriage should it be bestowed on you but never let it surpass your union with Me. I am always to be your first love for you are My first love and forever will be.

Letter 4: An Eternal Marriage ~ 25

Letter 5: Experiencing Heaven On Earth

In Your presence is fullness of joy;
At Your right hand are pleasures
forevermore.

Psalm 16:11

Letter 5: Experiencing Heaven On Earth

Dear Bride,

If you only knew how deeply I anticipate you coming to your home, heaven, to be with Me, your Bridegroom, for all eternity. How I wait with such longing in My heart. Yet, I do not wait in idleness nor do I want you to, for we can experience a heavenly union on earth by My precious Holy Spirit, now.

You do not need to wait until heaven to experience My touch, you can experience My glorious touch today. You do not need to wait until heaven to hear Me singing over you, open your heart and hear My voice singing over you, calling you unto Me this very moment. You do not need to wait until heaven to feel My breath, for My pneuma life fills your lungs even now.

You can experience My heavenly Presence as your Bridegroom now. As you do, you will be fulfilled and the longing to meet with Me as I have for you will deepen. The

Letter 5: Experiencing Heaven On Earth

yearning to be with Me in our home in heaven will only intensify the closer you draw to Me. This will intensify to such a degree that you will not be able to help but share this yearning and longing you sense for Me and I sense for you, My Bride, with others; so they too may encounter Me on this earth by My Spirit and enter a union that will last for all eternity.

Letter 6: How I See You

*You are altogether beautiful,
my love;
there is no flaw in you.*

Song of Solomon 4:7 (ESV)

Letter 6: How I See You

Dear Bride,

Do you know that I am captivated and mesmerised by you? That when I look at you, I see perfection? "How can this be?", you may wonder. You must know that when you gave your life to Me and became one with Me, you took on My very nature. We became one; so that what is in Me now is in you. You became a new creation. And how glorious is this new creation who I created you to be My Bride. How radiant! How spotless! How perfect! This is who you are. This is who I created you to be My Bride. I see no flaw in you.

"But why do I feel like I am dirty? Why do I feel inferior?", you may ask. When you look at yourself- your old fallen nature, it is true you will see the darkness, the sin, the filth. But you must remember My Bride, this is not who you are. This is not My Bride I betrothed unto Me, who will spend eternity with Me, whom I married and made a covenant union with. You are now separated from that sin and darkness and brought into My Light.

You are My glorious Bride without spot or wrinkle but you must see yourself this way. See yourself through My eyes and you will walk in how I see you. If you see yourself as an old creation, sin will enter and dominate. I did not marry your old sinful nature for your old self was crucified on the cross. I married you My Bride, My beautiful one, in all your splendour, in oneness with Me. Always remember, You are My Bride, there is no spot or flaw in you, for you and I are one.

Letter 7: Living As One

My beloved is mine, and I am his.

Song of Solomon 2:16

Letter 7: Living As One

Dear Bride,

Do you know what it means to forsake your life for Me? I am not telling you to give up all for no reason or for My amusement. We can only live in harmony in matrimony when your life and My life become one. You cannot function independently of Me, going in one direction when I am leading in another. How can two divided stand in agreement?

So for us to move together as one, there must be a letting go of your ways of doing things; a surrender of your will so that My ways and My will become yours, so that we may move as one. "How can this be? I am my own person", you may think. Yes, you are made of your own mind, will and emotions that function differently to the mind, will and emotions of any other I created. But you were made to surrender them all to Me, your Husband, so that I can lead us into My ways and plans for you.

Letter 7: Living As One

I want you to know that I am yours, My life is yours, but for you to experience My life as your own, your life must also be Mine - it is a mutual giving. I gave My life for you, I laid everything down so that you, by laying everything down too, could be made one with Me. Now we can move together in union, in fellowship, and in love. I am yours and you are Mine. My life is yours and your life is Mine. Together we are one.

Letter 8: Besotted By You

---

*You have captivated my heart,
my sister, my bride;
you have captivated my heart
with one glance of your eyes, with
one jewel of your necklace.
How beautiful is your love,
my sister, my bride!
How much better
is your love than wine...*

Song of Solomon 4:9-10 (ESV)

Letter 8: Besotted By You

Dear Bride,

When you see how much My gaze is upon you, how you always have My full attention, you will not look for attention and recognition from others.

My Bride, know that I am always thinking of you. Always, My heart is upon you. Always, you are on My mind. Eternally, you are in My heart. For you are the apple of My eye. The centre of My affection. You are My betrothed and I am deeply besotted by you.

My love for you is not like anything you can find in this world. It is a pure love, a holy love, an unconditional, selfless love.

I have your best welfare at heart. You can rest completely in My love for you, knowing I will take care of you. I will protect you. I cover you with My very life, My blood itself shed for you, that overcomes all that rises itself against you. You will never be in harm's way as you trust in Me your Bridegroom.

I cherish you and long to nurture you every moment, for you are My own and I am yours.

Letter 9: You Are My Bride

*And as the bridegroom rejoices
over the bride,
So shall your God rejoice over you.*

Isaiah 62:5

Letter 9: You Are My Bride

Dear Bride,

A truth I always want you to remember is this: You are My Bride. You are My Bride. Let the truth penetrate your heart. I see you as My Bride. This is how I want you to see yourself. This is who you are, you are My Bride.

A Bride is occupied and delights in her Bridegroom. He is the centre of her affection. And so it is for you. Let Me, your Bridegroom fill your heart to overflowing to be your deepest satisfaction. "How?", you may ask. Meditate on My love for you as your Bridegroom and soon your bridal love for Me will overflow in your heart by My Holy Spirit. Your love for Me is birthed in My love for you.

Remember, you are My Bride. I chose you and set you apart. You are My precious Bride and I love you with all My heart.

Letter 9: You Are My Bride ~ 45

Letter 10: My Kiss

Let him kiss me
with the kisses of his mouth-
For your love is better
than wine.

Song of Solomon 1:2

Letter 10: My Kiss

Dear Bride,

Oh, how I long to kiss you with the kisses of My mouth. But for Me to kiss you I need your heart to be still, gazing upon Me alone. How I long to kiss you My Bride, My darling.

Be still and drink in My love for you, My tender kisses as they melt your heart. Let My love and devotion overwhelm you as I shower you with My love. Let go of everything else and let Me kiss you.

This is My desire to kiss you, My Bride, to draw you so very close and for you to receive My tender affection towards you.

Will you still your heart and receive My tender kisses of love today?

Letter 10: My Kiss ~ 49

Letter 11: The Place Beyond Words

Though you have not seen him, you love him. Though you do not now see him, you believe in him and rejoice with joy that is inexpressible and filled with glory

1 Peter 1:8 (ESV)

Letter 11: The Place Beyond Words

Dear Bride

There is an inexpressible joy and glorious peace you will find in My love that goes beyond the human language. A depth of emotion you may experience in your heart beyond what you can articulate to another or have experienced before.

This is waiting for you now, here on earth. A place where words fall to the ground and all that is experienced is a divine exchange of bliss. I want to draw you into this place that is beyond words.

Come and enter the inexpressible wonder and joy of My love. Come away with Me, My Bride, and be swept up into another realm.

Come away with Me. I am waiting for you now.

Letter 11: The Place Beyond Words ~ 53

Letter 12: I Am Returning For You

"Then the kingdom of heaven shall be likened to ten virgins who took their lamps and went out to meet the bridegroom. And at midnight a cry was heard: 'Behold, the bridegroom is coming; go out to meet him!'

And the foolish said to the wise, 'Give us some of your oil, for our lamps are going out.' But the wise answered, saying, 'No, lest there should not be enough for us and you; but go rather to those who sell, and buy for yourselves.' And while they went to buy, the bridegroom came, and those who were ready went in with him to the wedding; and the door was shut. Afterward the other virgins came also, saying, 'Lord, Lord, open to us!' But he answered and said, 'Assuredly, I say to you, I do not know you.' "Watch therefore, for you know neither the day nor the hour in which the Son of Man is coming.

Matthew 25:1,6,8-13

Letter 12: I Am Returning For You

Dear Bride

Do you know I am counting down the days until our wedding feast? I am returning for you My Bride; coming for you, the one whom My heart desires and longs for so we may be together for all eternity. Be ready for Me My Bride, for surely I am coming quickly to this earth.

Be faithful to Me. Keep your eyes on Me. Be ready and waiting for Me, as I am ready and waiting for you.

Share My love and help others to be ready for Me but do not let the cares and entanglements of life ensnare you. Keep your heart fixed on Me and burning for Me in love, for My heart is forever fixed on and burning for you.

Prepare for My return by always walking in this truth: you are My Bride, and you are deeply loved by Me; I am yours and you are Mine

Let us be glad and rejoice and give Him glory, for the marriage of the Lamb has come, and His wife has made herself ready.

Revelation 19:7

Invitation To A New Life With Jesus

Jesus loves you so deeply and wants you to come closer in a beautiful bridal union with Him on this earth and for all eternity in heaven. But one thing separates you from having this relationship- sin.

The Word of God declares that we all have sinned and fall short of experiencing the glory of God (Romans 3:23) and that because of our sin, we are all deserving of hell (Romans 6:23). The only thing that can cleanse us from our sin and give us a new righteous life is the death and resurrection of Jesus.

> *For the wages of sin is death but the gift of God is eternal life in Jesus Christ our Lord.*
>
> Romans 6:23

Jesus, the Son of God, was perfect and without sin. He came down from heaven as a man and humbled Himself to die for your sins, being crucified on a cross. Three days later, He was raised from the dead, overcoming all the power of sin and darkness. Now, whoever believes in Jesus and turns from their sin unto Him, is forgiven and can enjoy an intimate relationship with God the Father, Son and Holy Spirit, now and for all eternity (John 3:16).

Through the sacrifice He made, Jesus wants to replace your old sinful life with the newness of His by the power of the Holy Spirit. This is what it means to be born again. You become a new creation born of God, and enter God's family. Your old life passes away, and all things become new (2 Corinthians 5:17).

It's not enough to simply believe Jesus exists. It doesn't matter if you have been to church your whole life or never before, the only way to come to know God and have a relationship with Him now and for all eternity is to turn away from your sin and surrender your whole life to Jesus.

Jesus is the only way to knowing God- now and for all eternity. If you want to accept God's invitation and receive this new life through what Jesus has done for you, pray the following prayer with all your heart:

Dear Jesus,

I believe You are the Son of God. Thank You for coming to earth to die and rise again for me.

I turn away from all my sin and surrender my life completely to You now. Come into my heart and cleanse me with Your precious blood. I receive Your forgiveness.

Jesus, You are now my Saviour and Lord. I belong to You- my heart is Yours forever and You are mine. God Almighty, You are my Heavenly Father and I am Your child. I am now born again!

Fill me with Your Holy Spirit. Holy Spirit, I give You permission to have Your way in every area of my life. Help me to live every day to please You God by the power You provide.

In Jesus name, I pray, Amen.

If you prayed this prayer with all your heart- congratulations! God's Word says that we must confess our faith in Jesus (Romans 10:9). If you prayed this prayer, I en-

Invitation To A New Life With Jesus ~ 65

courage you to tell someone (preferably someone who has a relationship with Jesus) about this eternal decision. Find a Spirit-filled local church, get baptised with water and the Holy Spirit (Matthew 3:11, Acts 1:5) and start reading God's Word, the Bible, to learn more about who God is- Father, Son, and Holy Spirit.

The fact that you have become born again into God's family does not mean that your life will suddenly be without problems. The difference is that now, regardless of what circumstances you face, you can be confident that Jesus loves you and empowers you to live every day in intimate oneness with Him. To help you walk this life, God the Father sent you the greatest gift on earth, the Holy Spirit, to be your personal Helper (John 14:26). Come now and embark on the most incredible journey of all- coming to know God, the Father, Son-Jesus, and Holy Spirit, and sharing their love with the world!

If you have just made this wonderful decision to give your life to Jesus, I would love to hear from you to encourage you. Please visit **www.KnowingGod.life** to connect and access further free resources.

Other Books By This Author

Heart of the Father
ebook available for free download on Apple bookstore

Heart of the Father -2

The Hidden Life and Beauty of Jesus: A 28 day devotional

Heart of the Holy Spirit: An action devotional

For more information or to contact the author visit: **www.KnowingGod.life**

68 ~ Other Books By This Author

www.ingramcontent.com/pod-product-compliance
Lightning Source LLC
Chambersburg PA
CBHW050446010526
44118CB00013B/1706